This man has got a big lorry.
The lorry is big. The lorry is new.
The lorry is red and yellow.
The man likes the red and yellow lorry.
He is happy this morning.

Look at my new lorry, says the man.
My lorry is new. What a good lorry.

The man is happy.

One morning the man jumps up
into the lorry.
He is going to the market.
He has got many mangoes.
He is taking the mangoes to
the market.

I am going to the market now, he says.

What is this?
Look at the new lorry.
The lorry is in the river.

Look at the man.
He is not happy now.

The man looks down.
Look at him. He is angry.

What can I do? he says.
My lorry is in the river.

The man jumps down out of the lorry.
He jumps into the river.
He is angry.

My lorry is in the river, he says.
What can I do?

The man is in the river with
the lorry.
He is wearing a white shirt.
The white shirt is dirty.

Have I got a rope? he says.

The man looks in the lorry.

Yes. Yes I have a rope here.
Good. Now I can pull my lorry
out of the river, he says.

The man pulls the rope.
He is pulling and pulling,
but he cannot pull the lorry
out of the river.

The man looks up. He is not happy.
He sees two small boys.
They are playing football.

Please come here. Do not go away.
Please come and pull my lorry
out of the river, says the man.

10

Which lorry? Who are you?
What do you want? the two boys say
to him.

My new red lorry is in the river,
says the man.
I have a rope, but I cannot
pull it out.

The boys say, We can go with you.
We can pull the rope for you.

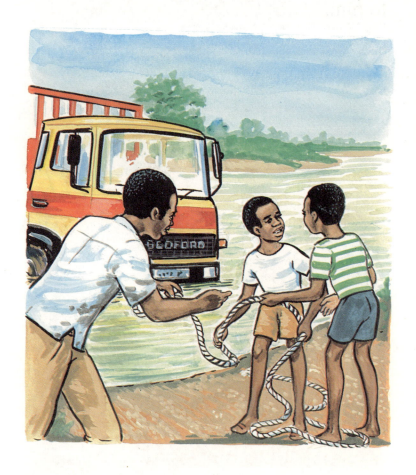

They all go to the river.
The red and yellow lorry is there.
Take the rope and pull it,
says the man.
One big pull, please.

They all take the rope.
The man pulls the rope,
and the two small boys pull the rope.

They are all pulling and pulling,
but they cannot pull the lorry
out of the river.

The man looks up. He is not happy.
He sees two big girls.
The two girls are looking at a book.

He says, Please come here.
Do not go away.
Please come and pull my lorry
out of the river.

14

Which lorry? Who are you?
What do you want? the girls say
to him.

My new red lorry is in the river,
says the man.
I have a rope, but I cannot
pull it out.

The two girls say, We can go
with you.
We can pull the rope for you.

They all go to the river.
The red and yellow lorry is there.
Now we can pull my lorry
out of the river.
Boys and girls, one big pull, please,
says the man.

The man pulls the rope,
and the two small boys pull the rope,
and the two big girls pull the rope.

They are pulling and pulling,
but they cannot pull the lorry
out of the river.

The man looks up. He is not happy.
He sees a teacher.
The teacher is going to school.

The man says, Please stop.
Do not go away.
Please come and pull my lorry
out of the river.

Which lorry? Who are you?
What do you want? the teacher says
to him.

My red and yellow lorry is in
the river, says the man.
I have a rope, but I cannot
pull it out.

The teacher says, I can go with you.
I can pull the rope for you.

Thank you, says the man.
Now one big pull.
Take the rope and pull, please.

The man pulls the rope,
and the two small boys pull the rope,
and the two big girls pull the rope,
and the teacher pulls the rope.

They are all pulling and pulling,
but they cannot pull the lorry
out of the river.

The man looks up. He is not happy.
He sees Father. Father is big.

The man says to Father, Please
come here.
Do not go away.
Please come and pull my lorry
out of the river.

Which lorry? Who are you?
What do you want? Father says to him.

My red and yellow lorry is in
the river, says the man.
I have a rope, but I cannot
pull it out.

Father says, I can go with you.
I can pull the rope for you.

Thank you, says the man.
Now one big pull.
Take the rope and pull, please.

The man pulls the rope,
and the two small boys pull the rope,
and the two big girls pull the rope,
and the teacher pulls the rope,
and Father pulls the rope.

They are pulling and pulling,
but they cannot pull the lorry
out of the river.

The man looks up. He is not happy.
He sees Mother.
Mother is going to the market.

The man says to Mother, Please stop.
Do not go away.
Please come and pull my lorry
out of the river.

Which lorry? Who are you?
What do you want? Mother says to him.

My new red lorry is in the river,
says the man.
I have got a rope, but I cannot
pull it out.

Mother looks at the man.
I can go with you.
I can pull the rope for you,
says Mother.

Thank you, says the man.
Now one big pull.
Please, all of you, one big pull.

The man pulls the rope,
and the two small boys pull the rope,
and the two big girls pull the rope,
and the teacher pulls the rope,
and Father pulls the rope,
and Mother pulls the rope.
They are all pulling and pulling.

Can we pull the red and yellow lorry
out of the river? they say.

Yes, yes we can pull the lorry
out of the river.
Look at it, they say.
It is coming out.

Pull, says the man. All of you, pull.
Pull please. Pull, pull.
The lorry is coming out of the river.

Look.

Mother is under Father,
Father is under the teacher,
the teacher is under the girls,
the girls are under the boys,
and the boys are under the man,
but the lorry is out of the river.

The red and yellow lorry is
out of the river.
It is not in the river now.

Thank you. Thank you all,
says the man.
Now I can go to the market.